Praise for
Swimming in Gilead

"[*Swimming in Gilead*] breaks the glass like a current, urgent version of Anne Sexton's *Transformations*. Cassie Premo Steele offers powerful affirmations of both self and connection in these poems, each page brimming with the clarifying forces of anger and wisdom and love. An inspiring, galvanizing collection."

Gayle Brandeis, author of *Drawing Breath:*
Essays on Writing, the Body, and Loss

~

"In *Swimming in Gilead*, [Cassie Premo] Steele weaves together poems of solace and hope. She offers you an incantation for survival and invites you to take a look within. Her poetry is like yoga: It will make you stretch and breathe toward a better version of yourself. Like her trees that 'reach' and 'learn as they teach,' these poems set at your feet a set of affirmations and mantras that guide you into calmness and peace. They provide a needed balm in these times of our modern day Gilead, where women's rights are being stripped away. These poems exhort you to live, live, live and fight, fight, fight. Simultaneously steeped in nature and our modern post-COVID world, the soul-affirming poems in this collection will center you."

Jennifer Bartell Boykin, author of *Traveling Mercy*
and Poet Laureate of the city of Columbia

~

Swimming in Gilead

by
Cassie Premo Steele

YELLOW ARROW
PUBLISHING
Baltimore, Maryland, USA

Contents

For my Gilead Sisters,
Colleen, Lantien, Mona, Shirley, Vanessa,
and Gilead Sisters everywhere

Acknowledgments

Reservoir Road, Issue 10, December 2022
"I Am (In Parts)"

Newberry Magazine, March/April 2023
"Under a New Moon"

SWIMMING IN GILEAD

Writing

Dawn is beginning.
You are a beginner.
Begin.
Within.

My hand with a pen.
Writing it down.
Rhythm.
Calm in heart and limb.

There is no end.
The story keeps going.
One word at a time.
Beyond mind.

We heal.
First, feel.
Insight.
First, write.

Writing is the teacher.
Beyond rules.
Stay in motion.
No priest or preacher.

Even roots move.
Stillness is illusion.
Answers do come.
Accept confusion.

Like a tree.
Reach.
Branches don't plan.
They learn as they teach.

Discover and dig.
Uncover. Deep.
Throw away what is done.
What is absent, keep.

Possession is impossible.
Motion.
Unstoppable.
Glee.

Fear is a signal.
Something is there.
Sit and listen.
Breathe. Air.

Rise.
Be a body again.
Nothing is forever.
Time is a friend.

Life.
Death.
Both.
And.

Use your hands.
Ask for a hand.
Take my hand.
Take a stand.

I Am (In Parts)

1/

I am pee and vomit, bad skin and old lemons.
I am pain and nausea, sick and sour. I am angry
but I can't express it as I wish because, like the sun,
I burn. I am hot without water or comfort. I am mean
and nuclear. I am my mother's anger and I hide in the
shade of it, afraid of admitting to it, and also being
this selfish and mean and caring only for myself and
not caring who I hurt and I hold it down, myself.
I am the one who does this to myself because
I was never allowed to see it or be it or say it.

2/

I am fuzzy sweaters and lip gloss, the pink part of me
that's feminine and nice. Makeup and wash your face.
Be quiet. Be good. You will get your reward in heaven.
Sacrifice. Offer it up. This is how we survive. It gives
the gift of patience, of waiting, of knowing what is risky,
when to hide. It is tougher than pink seems to be because
it's the color of my skin and this is vulnerable, and it takes
courage to let someone in. This is an authentic pink that is
not afraid to be afraid, not angry about anger, not
overwhelmed by overwhelm. A woman warrior.

3/

I am bright and bold. I come in green like leaves in spring
when everything sings, is new. I am delicate. I have many
tiny parts. I have traveled far. I am what shows when
I am not afraid to be fragile. I turn burnt orange in fall,
not red like fire because I have learned how to be beautiful
and sharp together. I am a glory, a celebration, a wind
rising, a desert in bloom after a century of doubt. I speak.
I listen. I take it all in. I am not afraid to let it all out.

4/

I am becoming who I dreamt of being all those years ago:
The girl by the pond, the girl in the trees, the young woman
who had her first period by the sea, the woman who wrote,
the one who studied and thought deeply, the woman who wanted
to be free, the one who loved mothering and the one who taught
transformatively, the woman who was bold enough to leave,
the one strong enough to regain her balance, the woman who
kept going, the one who believed, the woman who knew deep
down she had gifts for the world that would grow from her parts
because every part was a seed.

I Am Alive

I am alive and green
like the leaves of the dogwood tree
right in front of me
as I write
as I breathe
as I be.

I am grown and gone
like the seeds from the willow
that scattered like snow
so they could go
so they could know
so they could grow.

I am old and strong
like the bark of the oak
that shades our bed
through the dark parts
through the dream starts
through the heart.

I am grateful and small
like the grass under me
as I walk on my feet
wherever I leave
whatever I cleave
however I grieve.

I am still and shimmering
like the center of the sun
that loves us by burning
however we won
wherever we've come
whatever is done.

I am wise and watery
like the creek through the trees
that winds her way
to you
and you
and me.

I Am Healing

I am healing when I stop trying.
I am not saying it is easy.
I am sure to fail many times.

I am healing when I forget.
I am not saying it didn't happen.
I am sure, in fact, that it did.

I am healing when I am quiet.
I am not saying I am silent.
I am sure I have a voice.

I am healing when I speak.
I am not saying I don't listen.
I am sure, actually, I have a choice.

I am healing when I sit still.
I am not saying I will never go.
I am sure, always, I will grow.

Their Exasperation

After another summer storm,
they stepped out into sauna morning
to pick up branches from the ground
like dead bodies lying down.

Downtown there was a parade
with floats and fireworks
like a regular American day
until bullets ran astray.

These wombs are ours, they
want to say, but even words
are not free in this country
where fecundity is cut away.

Cunt is not enough to hold
what their tongues scream so bold,
and only breath can express
their exasperation at this dickish mess.

Stay or Go

The thing is that when faced with this question, it's not a question. When confronted with this choice, it's not a choice. We imagine it as such only when we are far removed from it. But when it happens to you, you know. You must go. That's always the decision you make. As much fear and terror as you have, the heartbreak and uncertainty, the regrets and wishing, and all the tears. You put one foot in front of another and go. Because the body can only take so much. Violence and yelling and hunger and shooting and air sirens and bombs and guns in the streets. After a time, the body sends a signal to the mind: Danger. Warning. Cannot cope. And so you go. You make the call. You get in line. You wait. You go. And you keep going. Just as every other immigrant, refugee, battered spouse, and abused child has done at one time or another. You are not alone. Meet us here on the road. We have more than enough food and fresh water that we can share with you. Together, we will welcome you to your new home.

Go

Walk the path where grasses grow
or take the crooked one with bare toes
or jump or crawl or run or go—
movement is not an option.
It's a lifelong collaboration.

Earth is a partner with gravity.
Everything learns to let go.
And we keep going after loss
and death and pain and this
yearning / split / gap inside.

Life begins in such a hole.
It crawls out to be born.
We are always being born.
We leave behind our torn
parts and become lizards.

This is not to say you won't
rest. Even the moon has
nights off. But keep going.
Go over barbed wires, under
fences, around the walls.

Sneak past the patrols.
Hide in the alleyways.
Your freedom is waiting.
Walk the path beyond hating.
Go to where long grasses grow.

How a Woman Goes

I never knew I was beautiful
until a woman wrapped
beads around my neck and
commanded me to breathe.
It came out wheeze and hard,
the tears like amber in me
that I'd never been able
to shed. I coughed like a
lunatic set free and laughed.
The body is a miracle, she said.
Each bead bloomed like a rose.
This is how a woman gets her name.

No matter how old we get,
we still need a mother.
Some women sever a limb
and make it a mother.
Other times we surrender
and are surrounded
by so many mothers
they are a constellation
of feed, nurture, grow.
And then we use our throats
to swallow. The beads rise and fall.
This is how a woman goes.

Other Things That Come and Go

Breath, of course. And the body.
Whether we are walking or
living or dying. It doesn't stay.
The day. Each night, it goes away.
Night, too. Swallowed by light
every morning. Rain. Sun. Clouds.
Wind. Let us not neglect the
waves. Such endless motion.
And yet still calm. On and on.
And you. You come in. You
go out. No judgment. No
regret. This is the way of all
things. It is the sign of living.

The Woman Speaks of Bicycles

I've known bicycles:
I've known bicycles new as my skin and older than my dried blood
from my womb.

I've known bicycles:
Reliable rubber and metal bicycles.
My body has grown strong like bicycles.

I rode along the Minnesota roads when constant motion was my freedom.
I got off my bike and walked the sugar bluffs, puffing with each step.
I looked upon the Mississippi and had a vision of finally flowing away.
I heard the wheels of my bike whizzing downhill at the end of the day.

I've known bicycles:
Reliable rubber and metal bicycles.
My body has grown strong like bicycles.

I rode in Carolina when children waited for me back home.
I got off my bike and walked the hilly edge of Covenant Road.
I looked upon the Congaree River and knew I would always stay.
I heard the music of my own voice saying I could live a different way.

My body has grown strong like bicycles.

The Year of Lists

We wrote lists of groceries and things
we needed for the house and skin,
lists of chores to complete, reminders
of calls to make and things to take in,
lists of medicines and their times,
symptoms and their intensity,
lists of memories we almost forgot
that came back to us in the night.

We wrote lists until we didn't, when
everything went online, even shopping
happened without handwriting,
the toilet paper and the lotion lying
next to the apples and rice on the porch,
the medicines coming in the mail,
the chores suddenly pared down to
dusting and the endless dishes.

We wrote lists in our head then,
restaurants we missed, people
we'd kissed who were now dead,
until the lists got so long that we had
to erase daily what had gone wrong,
we had to press our palms against
the screen and call this love and work,
blending friendship and collegiality.

We wrote lists again after some time,
released like inmates from our own
homes, and once more picking up
dog food seemed like a necessary
chore to do, and we wondered how
many of our neighbors who were
still alive had been sick, and we prayed
at every sniffle and allergy and flu.

We wrote lists of what mattered when,
after a whiskey or two, late at night,
we were no longer alone: Breath,
trust, touch, laughter, breath again—
and our tears came down then
like a list of all we could not say,
like what was here one day and
gone the next. Gone, gone away.

Time's Up

There is an inner clock
in my veins, and I stop
when the alarm goes
off and stand still to
see what is happening—
nervous and watching,
I wait for a notification
of another incidence of
gunshots and bodies
falling and innocent
people falling down
and dying off. We are
going extinct as summer
heat is unrelenting and
wildfires keep raging
and first responders
are on the scene
but few are surviving and
there is no escape from
the destruction we keep
reaping season after season,
and I try to press
snooze on the clock
of my body, but the
alarm won't stop,
and my only hope is
that you are here and
hear the sirens, too.

I Will Wear a Mask for You

I will put on makeup and smear it
Or wear no makeup and to hell with it
I will get little lines behind my ears
Or keep adjusting my hair over there
I will be glad I don't smoke anymore
Or wish I had something like it again
I will miss seeing your smile in the store
Or be mad that he can't see my scowl
I will hope that I don't infect you
Or be relieved when I stay well
I will breathe deeply back in the car
Or leave it on when it's cold
I will remember to brush my teeth
Or smell the last food I've eaten
I will try to envision this as over
Or surrender to this new normal
I will admire women who match it
Or sigh at the marketing on it
I will worry when you don't do it
Or let go into the inevitability of it
I will never run out without it
Or stop taking one on a run
I will burn them in a fire one day
Or tuck one as a souvenir away
I will see it as an old love letter
Or pray that our enemies get better

Let Us Let Go

Let us let go of stuff, the art we kept out of fear or status,
the junk, Post-It notes and reminders to self that are on
an app now, the books we read once and didn't love,
or never read and never want to, the presents and cards
that meant something at the time, the things your mother
gave you to keep because she no longer wanted them,
but you don't really either, the notes from classes you
don't need because you've taught them so many times
you can do it in your sleep, the envelopes you thought
you'd use, the free bookmarks: How many bookmarks
can you really use at once anyway?

                         And keep these:
Photos, how little they were, how young you were,
how classy they were, how afraid you were, how happy
they were, how inexperienced about everything you were.

     The journals, arranged by year, peek inside
just long enough to remember the seasons:
Depression, dissertation, motherhood, striving,
love, learning,
                     and eventually leaving each one behind.

Let us let go of the year even as we embrace what is no longer
here: The dead who still care, the work that is done,
the dreams we had and woke from, the selves we were
on the way to becoming a completely new one.

Marriage Equality

Love is love and lays
herself down for lips
and skin and thighs
and the orange peel
wrinkle of small
and secret places inside.

Love is not a breaking,
not something hurt,
not cracked or chipped
nor lacking any pieces.

Love is full and filling,
a deep breath opening,
that tear afterward
falling, and the yes
of being together
even when alone.

Love is the drumbeat
to the songs of
chrysalis and seed,
storm and spring,
letting go to welcome
summer heat.

Love is sweet like just
shucked corn, ending
with the drip of watermelon,
fresh on our tongues,
under blue sky.

Love brings autumn water
to usher in the next
weather when one season
is ready to be torn.

Love is pump and touch,
engine and combustion, burst and
beginning, a volcano
from which life is born.

Volcano Woman

Proud, out, loud,
Fire, feisty, you
Woman of waves,
Lava and magma

Hot liquid running
Down fine breasts,
Spilling wet over
Pubic bone beach

Into the ocean
Where fish are
Swimming and singing,
Praise and preach

I want you
To teach me
How to sleep
Between each eruption.

Her Answer to Gen X

Oh, generous one, gender,
so fluid and shifting,
one moment a mushroom
standing up in the damp ash,
the next an ocean rolling
over red rocks until crash.

Oh, genres, so many!
Poetry and story,
research and song,
essay and aphorism,
each with its form,
allowing multiplicity
of voice and vision,
endlessly being born.

Oh, generations past
and those to come,
the ones here with us
now and babies waiting
with grannies gone,
collecting knowledge
in a woven basket,
ready to pass on.

Oh, genius, the spark
of mind that writes
and grows, shares
and knows, loves
us all abundantly,
fearlessly, generously.

Flower, Fly, Catch

i. flower

I was an orange lotus bed, a bed
for bodies to rest and be blessed,
make love and make life. There was beauty in the shining
light of my closed petals, the veins ran through
with liquid that was warm and sighed.

But I was not open. I was tight. As lovely as that flower was,
it was frozen. Afraid, still, made so by what might happen again
that had once long ago happened and I'd worked so hard
to relieve and release and relax and it was all hard,
hard work, great trying, and never really letting go or letting in or
letting be.

It was an internal mountain I forged all by myself,
daily, and I told myself I didn't need a sherpa, I was fine all by
myself.

ii. fly

I could fly. I'd learned to whiz by with my wings
in glittering iridescence, I could go forward and backward
and make loops and figure eights, and the shapes
of my flight drew all kinds of astonishing things.

Until I fell. And flat on my back, my tail feathers en masse
and my beak overturned, I lay there, wondering why
this had happened and the pain was so great,
and I could not even move, and all of the trying was useless.

iii. catch

It was one of my own petals, I realized, that caught me.

My Lifelines

Sometimes I am drowning
in a lake of my own making.
It is I who turned
on the taps before bed,
I who dumped everything
from the freezer to melt,
I who opened the windows
when storms were stirring,
I who poured the whiskey
and wine on the floor.

Crying out for help, I take
off my life vest and tie
my hands behind my back
and stuff boulders into
my bra (but not in that
precise order, obviously).

And then I laugh because
my lifelines are in my own
hands, I've always known
that, and what I really
want is company,
someone to fix a leaky
pipe for me, or watch the
weather report, or eat
my defrosted dinner, or
toast to our life together.

And you, yes, you have
always been there, you
are with me all the time,
and all I have to do is
to pay close attention
to this life of mine.

Trees Have a Lap

You must crawl into them
to feel it. They don't call it
that. The tree word is
branches. And leaves are,
in their language, hands.

Their lap has a song. Each
one is different. Pines sing
about nesting and letting
go of cones. Oaks say, Wait.
River birches say, Go deep.

Once, I didn't look where
I was going, and I tripped
over my own roots. It's quite
embarrassing but common.
Willow helped me out.

It happens when we doubt,
she said. The rhythm of trunk
gives way. We fall, fell, are
felled. It's a whole conjugation.
A history of nations.

I learned the courage
of trees. I dropped not
only what I didn't need,
but also my arms and
hands and legs and feet.

I was felled. But really,
I felled myself. The trees
told me this transpires.
They said there are always
roots and new shoots.

My hands came back
green. They smelled
like ocean water. They
were incredibly clean.
I knew I could start over.

This Is How We

I once knew a Native woman,
Eastern Cherokee, who taught me
that in order to fix a rip in a basket,
you can't just go in after it.
You have to unwind the fibers until
it's pinestraw and sweetgrass again.
This is how we begin again.

I once injured my left knee
and the physical therapist,
a Latina from Texas, showed
me how a lack of stability
in my right hip had caused it.
The body crosses like this,
she said. It's all connected.
This is how we heal again.

I once lay on my bed for hours
on end, as a child in Minnesota,
reading book after book while
my body disappeared, and so
did the pain and fear, until
I was just a mind in a story.
It took me years to invite
my body back into the party.
This is how we move again.

I once stayed in endless motion
of serving and cleaning, cooking
and feeding, wiping and washing,
drying and folding, until my mind,
always so strong, broke hard
and long, and for the first time,
I told the truth in therapy.
This is how we feel again.

I once heard a song that felt
like it was singing all that had
gone wrong, and I thought
it had been written just for
me, and then a pandemic broke
the globe and I realized everybody
knows the melody of tragedy.
This is how we begin to be together for the first time really.

Brazen

I blaze then.
In my fire.
From the tip.
Follow it down.
Be here then.
Hot, hotter, hottest.
Open to knowing.
Me in you.
You in me.
The rage, see.
I own it.
It owns me.
It flows so.
It grows me.
Magma, lava, volcano.
Foam and heat.
See down below.
What comes out.
Devours only me.
This is it.
The point then.
Where I go.
Or you do.
We make we.
After burns us.
We are these.
Soil and green.
Come new trees.
Kiss me hard.
Pull my roots.
Water my shoots.
Touch my leaves.
Hand petal me.

Feel the soft.
Smell the clean.
Nature's laundry day.
This fresh breeze.
Caress my skin.
Warm the frozen.
February fire chat.
Talk to me.
Whisper, reason, scream.
Make any sound.
Take me down.
Below the dirt.
In the ash.
Watch me rise.
Like light, ignite.
Like dawn, emerge.
Take sun flight.
Give holy urge.
I am brazen.
Be brazen, too.
Brazen with me.

Dialogue

This is the last day of your life, the bomb said.
But I've only just begun, the child said.

That may be true, the bomb responded.
But I can't hear you.

-

This is the last cake you will ever eat, said the jailer.
But I will get out one day, said the inmate.

Will you? the guard asked.
I have to believe, the prisoner answered.

-

This is the last breath I will take, said the body.
But I will live on, said the soul.

Will you? asked the body.
No one really knows, said the mind.

-

I know, said the soul.

Love Speech

Hey there, can I help you carry that?
Yes, let me. Take it. From your hands.

Open your hands now. Take this cup.
I will fill it up. Please. Let me.

Oh, I almost forgot!
I have a gift for you. No, stop.

Open it now. I'm glad you like the box.
But look inside. Yes, it's seeds.

You can plant them wherever
you need beauty. Or shade.

Or something sweet.
A scent. A fruit to eat.

Why? Because I love you.
No, really. I mean it.

There is no one closer to you than me.
I got your back. No crying necessary.

Help Me, My Body Said

She wasn't as direct as this.
She didn't use words, let alone lips.
She didn't even use her hands
like in some game of charades.

She didn't pick up a pen.
Or put a message on paper.
Her missive was indirect.
But no less intentional.

Help me, she said, with breathlessness.
Help me, she said, with racing heart.
Help me, she said, with joint pain.
Help me, she said, with a mind gone blank.

How? I asked her.
Then I called my doctor.
And another and another
and another.

Take this pill.
Take this test.
Take your blood.
Take your rest.

My body's engine light kept flashing.
So I took my foot off the gas.
Pulled to the side of the road.
Threw my keys in the grass.

Drank some gin.
Got drunk off my ass.
The next morning, it was all a blur.
But there was a chair.

I sat in it.
And I started speaking.
I used my words.
And lips.

I used my hands when language slipped.
I picked up a pen.
I wrote on paper.
I was direct. I tried to be.

First, this happened, I said.
And then, that happened.
What are you talking about?
asked my body.

Someone opened a deep grave, I said.
Bad things came out.
They'd been there since before I had words.
I tried to run from the monsters.

The monsters were me.
So I tried to run from myself.
But I missed me when I was away.
So I sat down and said, Come get me.

And the monsters floated away.
Like balloons.
Like bubbles.
Like the pain.

Railway Queen

Seven years ago (it seems longer, but it isn't so),
I met myself on the road. You don't believe me.
But I'll go ahead and tell you anyway. It happened
by the railway. As you know, it runs behind the
house, keeping time with cargo from China and
lumber and oil and an occasional passenger
train in the dead of night. There's no river there,
but a little creek flows when there's been rain,
and herons and egrets have come to claim it
as home, and it was here in the darkness by
the makeshift riverbed that I met her. She looked
like a queen, which is to say, I didn't recognize her
as myself. Her hair was longer, her body less curvy,
and there was a calmness about her as if her nerves
were closed for vacation. I took a long look, then
looked away because I didn't want her to think
me rude for staring, but the truth was her face
was as compelling as a full moon on my third
glass of wine. She was that fine. And later, after
she told me what she'd come to tell me, when
I was back in my bed, properly wed to my wife—
we were newlyweds then, and each night held
promise—I realized that it had been me I'd seen:
A future me, an older me. More serious because
she'd held her pains in the soft skin of her own
palms and learned not to crush them or throw
them away but let them sit there like baby birds
still growing their wings. I fell asleep at dawn
and I was smiling. I was equally amazed and afraid
by what I had seen. And when I woke to the fullness
of sun, I felt an invisible crown on the top of me
because it was me who was the railway queen.

Crone Rain

There is a small crossroad
just beside my bed
where on a dark night
I placed my foot and fled.
I was a woman then.
Now I am an empty sack
of yarn and thread.
My fingers became needles.
I can create from my head
whatever will keep me warm,
soft and secure, and not dead.
I light a candle before dawn
and pray for an escape.
I am my own railroad.
My bathrobe became a cape.
When you hear the rain at night,
you will triumph the next day.
Freedom comes to wombs
who refuse to be locked away.

Sun Loving

Just before the day ends, I look up
and the sun is in drag, orange lipstick
and purple fingernails, red hair,
peach high heels, and I say, Hey, girl,
where you headed? And she says,
Off to bed. Alone? I ask. You know
better than that, she laughs, and
as she sashays away, I see the moon
and stars take her by the hand
and lead her downstairs to a ballroom
for a final dance before kisses and
all the love she has ever deserved.

Love Letter to My Head

In there, unseen, you walk the ramp
without fashion or designer heels.

You spin and all synapses stand,
applaud for what you do within.

My head, my brain, my unique way
of seeing hearing thinking saying:

You are unlike any before or after
and even while sleeping you are

The director scriptwriter producer star
and there is love loss drama survival.

You never give in even when buried.
There are shovels you draw in your journal.

You move dirt around and come back
from the dead easily, will never go silent.

Toothpaste

I read a poem
by a poet
with a mother

    this is how poetry begins

her pain
is not really
her pain

    and this is how story ends

when I was young
love was
sweet candy

    this is what I wanted

I am old enough now
to love
the clean of toothpaste

    and this is what wisdom is

Under a New Moon

Plant something.
Flowers. Crops.
An intention.

You have the power to begin again.

She sees you.
The moon, I mean.
Your cycles are visible.

You can rest assured that you are seen.

Rain is coming.
Don't water too soon.
Just a drink.

The roots are delicate and need space.

Watch the moon.
How she grows.
You can do this, too.

Even when you are staying in one place.

Then she is full.
Pregnant with herself.
It happens regularly.

You can give birth with a little help.

Storms will come.
Seek shelter.
Cover the seedlings.

Destruction is part of every equation.

And then let go.
You don't need to cling.
Release what you know.

This is how all learning happens.

Hope shines at night.
Wait for dreams.
Listen to the light.

This is when new ideas will come.

Wait three nights.
Have faith.
You are not alone.

Over and over, start again.

Darkness grows.
Rest. Rest. Rest.
Growth is deep below.

You must learn to abandon clinging.

You have another chance.
The moon says this is so.
Now go.

Under a Full Moon

What must be done is a gathering
of women under a full moon,
each one holding in her hands
a leaf or bud or flower, blade
of grass, and together we say
the names of these plants,
and the list transforms into
a poem, a prayer, a spell, an
incantation, a chant and belief
in peace, peace, peace, peace.

And when our throats go sore
and voices tire, we take our
empty hands and make a chain
to keep the violence from crashing
into bodies any longer and
dream that war will cease.

No Certainties

Nothing is certain
but still tomorrow comes.
What leads to love
is today's curtain.

My anger pulls
the curtain back
on what I did
or did pretend.

I am learning
to put strange truths
on the stage
and watch them ripen.

Apples pears oranges
figs grapes blueberries
cherries plums apricots:
I am all these women.

Sweet fruit flesh
fills our heads
with mouths open
and ears tasting.

We speak.
We listen.
We survive.
We survive.

Seeds

I spent years diving and digging
and bringing coral and diamonds
up into the light with my palms,
but the sun had dimmed so much
that my gifts were invisible, and I
mourned the bodies and voices
of women and girls I'd wanted
to crown with orange and bright
jewels who had all gone down
underground in a collective action
of mutual survival, and so I let
what I wanted to give away
drop to the ground and walked
so long up a mountain that I could
look back and see the seeds had
buried themselves back into the
earth to be trees. Tall were their
trunks, and the leaves sang green
songs to bring the girls and women
back to me and back into the castles
and courts we ruled over again in
this land where we'd always belonged.

Tuesday Afternoon

I walk with my fingers on the page and
I dance with my hips on the stage I have
made in my room where bluebirds take
turns with me playing the parts of star
and audience and I hear the silence filled
with breath and electric hum and a neighbor's
rake and I touch my dog's fur and think
about origins and species and know that
nothing the mind does brings as much joy
as an animal can and I laugh while
remembering my grandson's voice after he
knocked my chin with a stick in the garden
and asked me, Are you okay, Gaga?
and I wonder what would have happened
if God had been more like this boy in Eden
and instead of rules and banishment, we'd
been met in our mistakes and our pain
with a question and compassion.

Tuesday Night

The sun bleeds peach tea,
and the mother tree lights
her leaves and drips yellow
sweet from cups as the day
goes belly up and asks to be
scratched, and I say, Good day,
good day, to her, as she settles,
and the stars start to stir while
Venus shines a mirror
and I say beauty
and Jupiter throws dice
and I say luck and
moon, who is just a
nearer star, really,
glows lights from above
onto the skin of my body
I'm in tonight and for once,
I do not worry about
time as I say love.

Leaves and Straw

I am in love with pigs.
The ones with leaves and straw
who survived the wolf, his breath,
and ran to their sister with bricks.

I am also in love with a wolf.
The one who cross-dressed
to save their life, myopic and
melancholy, moody and so hungry.

I am in love with a giant.
The gentle gardener who grew
his own escape hatch to a
safe patch without bullies.

I am in love with a girl.
The one who was so picky
about a chair and was a champ
of empty houses and midday naps.

I am in love with five kittens.
Those mittens were unnecessary
on twenty paws anyway.
I bake them pies every day.

Her Tarot Reading

The significator is a woman on fire.
Burn the papers.
Burn the past.
Don't burn out.
You are here to last.

What is passing away is doubt.
Scream.
Shout.
Say it out loud.
You don't deserve that crowd.

What is arriving is water.
Swim.
Float.
Let yourself flow.
Be your own boat.

What is above is the sun.
Smile.
Dance.
Light up with fun.
You are nowhere near done.

What is below is a rock.
Stand.
Sit.
Balance the move and the stop.
You are already on top.

She Walks Two Worlds

She walks two worlds when she walks,
one foot on earth and the other in sky.
Her mind is the balance where feathers
fly, off and on, depending on the weather
or the storms in her heart. She is a tightrope
walker, a trapeze artist, a daredevil
kissed by angels. She sleeps midday rocked
by the lullabies of hawks. She speaks
in the dark to the moon and keeps
her secrets locked in a pastel room.
She creates waves with eyelashes and
composes symphonies with plastic glasses
and she loves the sound of silence
above everything, the way the breath
rings in the bell tower of her chest.
Her heart is different from the rest.
It feels with an intensity that leaves
the word courage breathless.
Her body is the interpreter of languages
between earth and sky, and every line
is part of a poem she is writing as she
walks, her feet rising and falling, her
steps beginning and ending, her body
living and dying, in this world where
beauty is another word for goodbye.

Okefenokee

May you wake with hawk
singing in the longleaf green
a praise song to our sun
who rises to make life seen.

Your first breath is smooth
and hangs heavy in the air
like Spanish moss in scrub oak
and fingers through your hair.

The coffee we made is warm
like the river tannin brown,
and you sip it slowly
as barred owl soars down.

Later I will touch your skin
like dragonflies land
with red and yellow and blue
wings upon my hand.

Our fears lie underneath
with alligator eyes,
but we paddle with courage
and love side by side.

Hawk lands by my feet
then returns to the tree.
Woodpecker taps out joy
for another year of you and me.

Age

Your blooming face has petals of gray now,
and your leaves are more wrinkled and drier,
but you are still the flower I found on the
roadside singing like a daisy, and I almost
walked by but didn't, and the seeds we
watered together have grown and flourished,
and we see the next generations coming
into sweet fruit alongside our old roots,
too, and every morning, I sing a song of
gratitude: Thank you, thank you, thank you.

Let Us Begin Again

Be very quiet. Make it dawn.
Rise from bed. Walk on the lawn.
Wait for it. The sun is coming.
It's a new one. It's beginning.
You don't believe me, you say
this happens every day, there's
nothing new under the sun and
certainly not the sun itself.
Put your doubts on a shelf,
I say to you. Hush now.
Listen to the birds singing.
Watch the blue ones feeding
their babies. See the heron
heading south for fishing.
Look at the egrets catching
pink light in their white wings.
Faith is made of things like
these, everyday movements,
sights and sounds that you
usually ignore, and today,
since you've told me you're
tired of life and wanting something
more, I've shown you how to do it,
and now that you know,
come, let us begin again.

Six Things the Feather Taught Me

1. Everything lands.
   Even the majesty and beauty
         of sky-born power
         comes down.

2. Everything can be found.
   Even the dropped and discarded
         and fallen to the ground
         is picked up.

3. Everything matters.
   No matter how light or slight,
         all matter weighs something.
         You matter, too.

4. Everything finds a home.
   A nest or grass or goblet,
         no better than or worse.
         We all rest.

5. Everything holds magic.
   The unexpected and expected,
         the good news and bad.
         Especially that.

6. Everything has meaning.
   We make it on our own wings.
         We fly through things.
         We keep going.

Declaration

I declare deeply that I am free
      in my mind,
despite the weight
I find there sometimes, telling
        me to serve and care and take
           a load I cannot shake.

I am no handmaid.

I tell you that.

My independence comes from me,
      this body, breathing, skin open
         and bones moving.
I love what brings me life
      and sever ties with strife
         of woman, vessel, chalice, bowl.

I've come too far to let them lock me up in part or whole.

Grieve. Rage. Cry. Shout.

Every sound from my mouth
      is sacred, holy prayer.
         I am the priest and the power.

Swimming Deeper
into *Swimming in Gilead*

To enhance your exploration of the themes in *Swimming in Gilead*, you might want to answer these questions in a journal, which can be very healing and empowering. You might also use them as starting points for discussions with friends or in a book club.

A special thanks to all the women writers I've had the honor to teach over the years who have helped me understand poetry as a dialogue, and my hope is that you, too, might find yourself writing poetry in response to these questions.

****

"Writing"
> What would it mean for you to 'take a stand'?

"I Am (In Parts)"
> How are you learning to see your parts as 'seeds'?

"I Am Alive"
> Complete the sentence with a poem of your own: "I am . . ."

"I Am Healing"
> In what ways have you grown recently?

"Their Exasperation"
> Complete the sentence: "My anger is . . ."

"Stay or Go"
> When was a time you had to leave?

"Go"
> What does freedom mean to you?

"How a Woman Goes"
> Who has mothered you?

"Other Things That Come and Go"
    What have you allowed to go?

"The Woman Speaks of Bicycles"
    How have you grown strong?

"The Year of Lists"
    In what ways did the pandemic change you?

"Time's Up"
    How does climate change affect your life?

"I Will Wear a Mask for You"
    Write a love letter to an enemy.

"Let Us Let Go"
    Who are you on the way to becoming?

"Marriage Equality"
    How do you define love?

"Volcano Woman"
    Write a love letter to your body.

"Her Answer to Gen X"
    How has growing older made you 'love . . . abundantly'?

"Flower, Fly, Catch"
    What have you learned from illness?

"My Lifelines"
    List seven things you love about your life.

"Trees Have a Lap"
    In what ways have you learned to 'start over'?

"This Is How We"
    What have you learned about healing?

"Brazen"
    What does brazen mean to you?

"Dialogue"
    How is your soul in a dialogue with you now?

"Love Speech"
    In what ways is it difficult for you to accept help?

"Help Me, My Body Said"
    What is your body saying to you?

"Railway Queen"
    Write about a recent dream you've had.

"Crone Rain"
    How are you claiming your freedom?

"Sun Loving"
    What do you deserve that you are not getting?

"Love Letter to My Head"
    How are you ready to stop being silent?

"Toothpaste"
    What is your definition of wisdom?

"Under a New Moon"
    In what ways are you taking a chance right now?

"Under a Full Moon"
    Write about one way you work toward peace.

"No Certainties"
    How have you survived?

"Seeds"
    What does 'mutual survival' mean to you?

"Tuesday Afternoon"
    What in you is asking for compassion?

"Tuesday Night"
    How do you honor the close of the day?

"Leaves and Straw"
    Write about your favorite story from childhood.

"Her Tarot Reading"
    What would it mean for you to 'be your own boat'?

"She Walks Two Worlds"
    What two worlds do you walk?

"Okefenokee"
    Where have you traveled to find love?

"Age"
    What has changed about how you view aging?

"Let Us Begin Again"
    How are you beginning again right now?

"Six Things the Feather Taught Me"
    What have you learned from a gift from nature?

"Declaration"
    Write your own declaration of freedom.

Cassie Premo Steele, PhD, is a lesbian ecofeminist poet and novelist and the author of 18 books. *Swimming in Gilead* is her seventh book of poetry. Her poetry has won numerous awards, including the Archibald Rutledge Prize named after the first Poet Laureate of South Carolina, where she lives with her wife. Find out more at cassiepremosteele.com.

Thank you for supporting independent publishing.

Yellow Arrow Publishing is a nonprofit supporting writers and artists identifying as women. Visit YellowArrowPublishing.com for information on our publications, workshops, and writing opportunities.